Mel Bay's Modern
Technique Solos
GUITAR METHOD
GRADE 6

by William Bay

Table of Contents

Prelude *(Bach-Bay)* 5

Prelude *(Carcassi)* 8

Blues Triplet *(Bay)* 8

Andante in Bm *(Bay)* 9

Allegro Brillante *(Carcassi)* 10

Meditation *(Carcassi)* 13

Allegro *(Carcassi)* 14

Study #2 *(Carcassi)* 16

Prelude in C Minor *(Carcassi)* 19

Study #5 *(Carcassi)* 20

Prelude #5 *(Molino)* 22

Etude in G Minor *(Carcassi)* 25

Le Petite Moulin *(Saint-Saëns)* 26

Study #1 *(Volpe)* 30

Study #8 *(Carcassi)* 34

Study #15 *(Carcassi)* 36

Study #22 *(Carcassi)* 41

Narcissus *(Nevin)* 44

Prelude

Moderato
Bach-Bay
- throughout
p

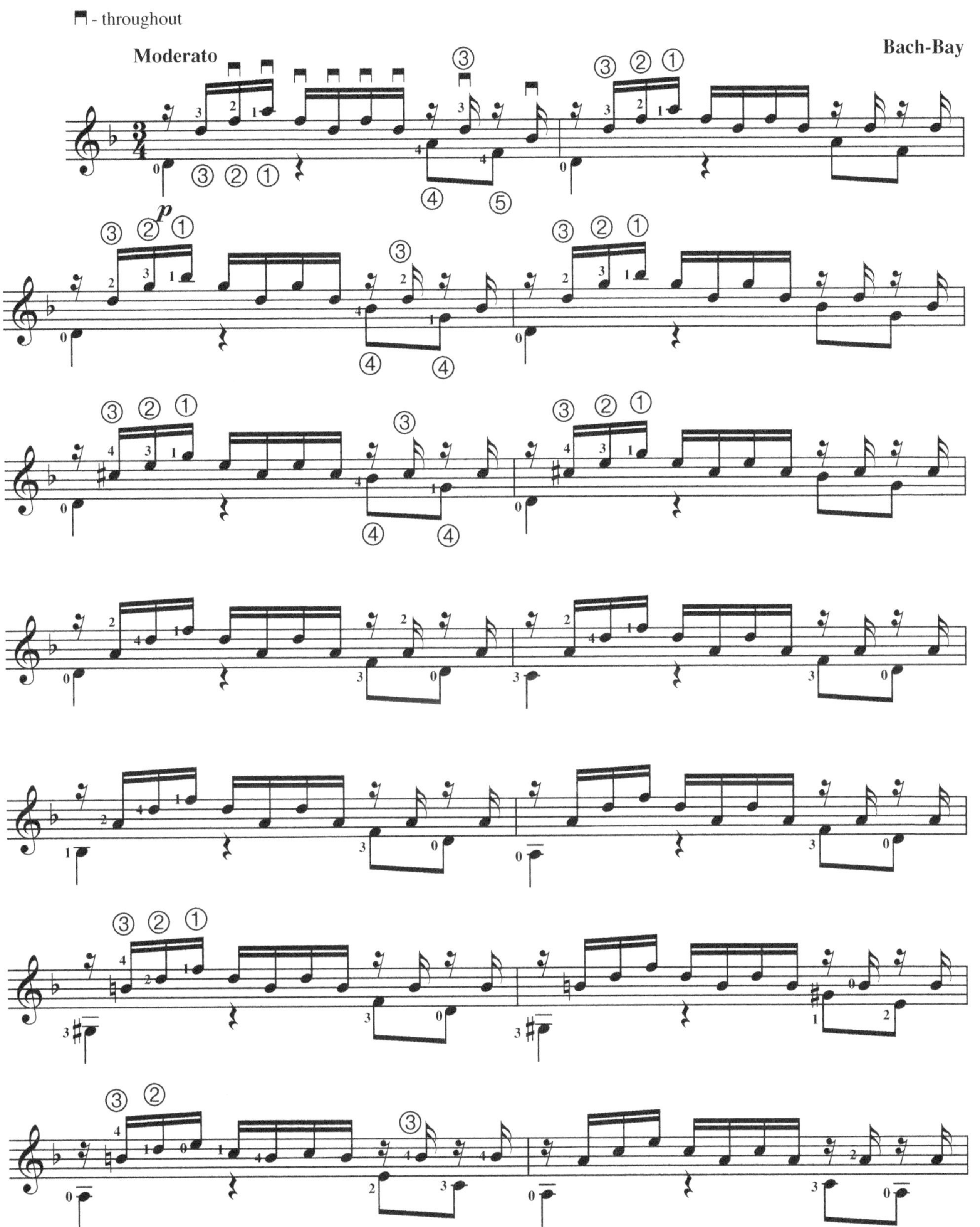

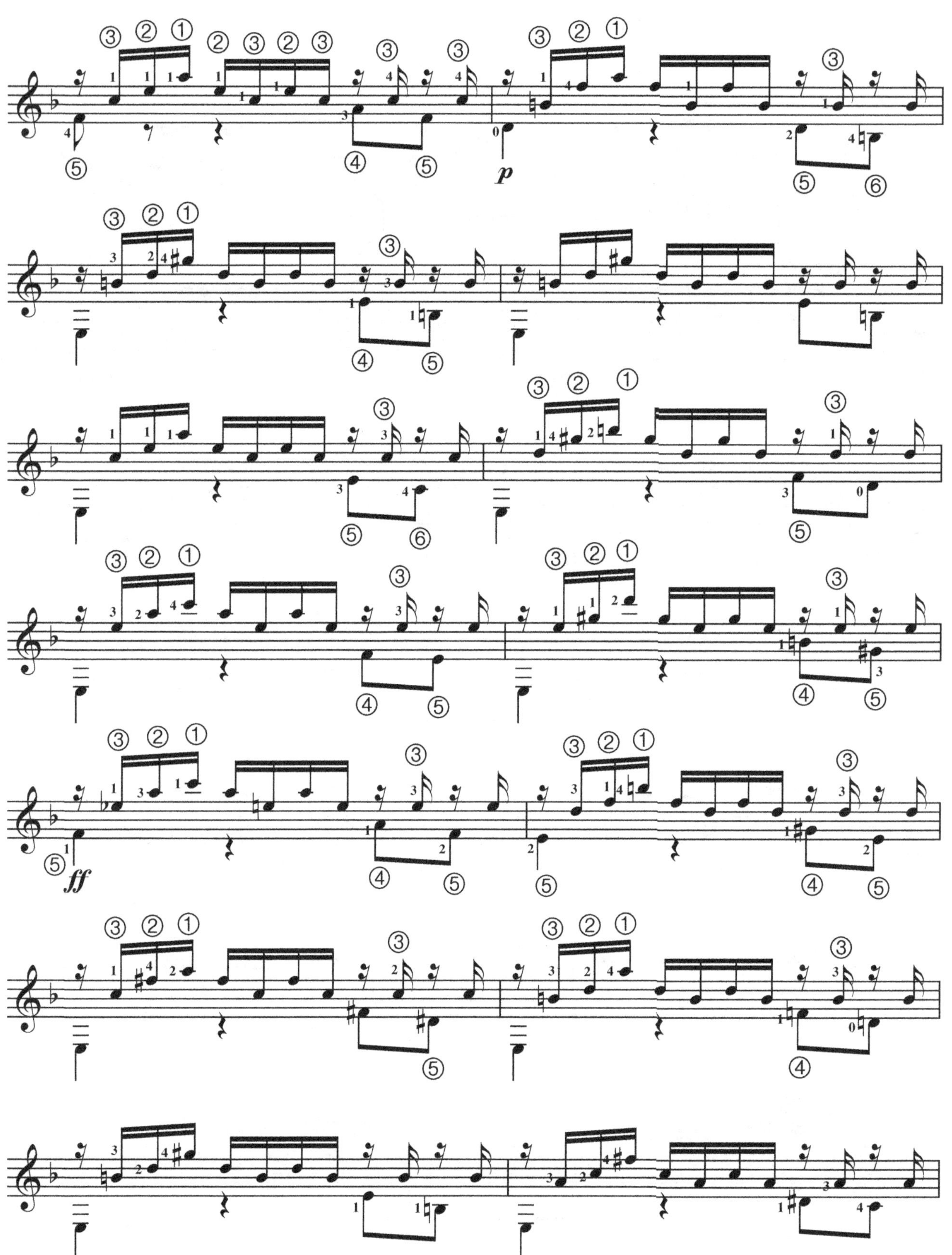

Prelude

Slowly **Carcassi**

Blues Triplet

Bill Bay

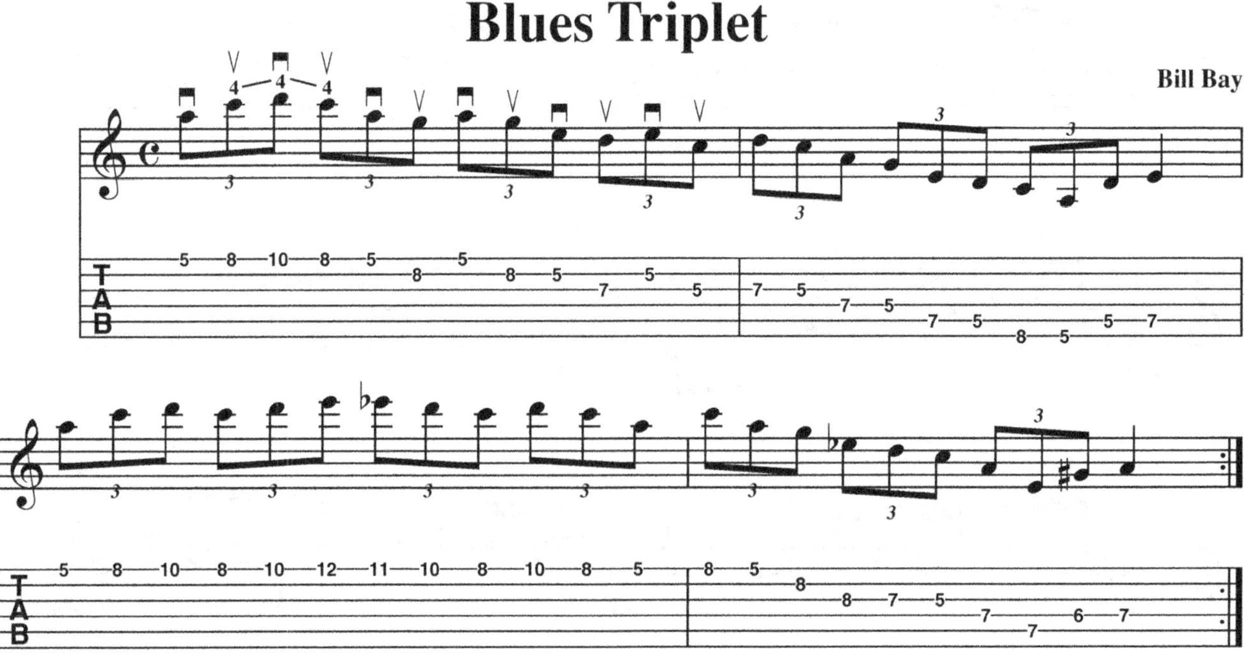

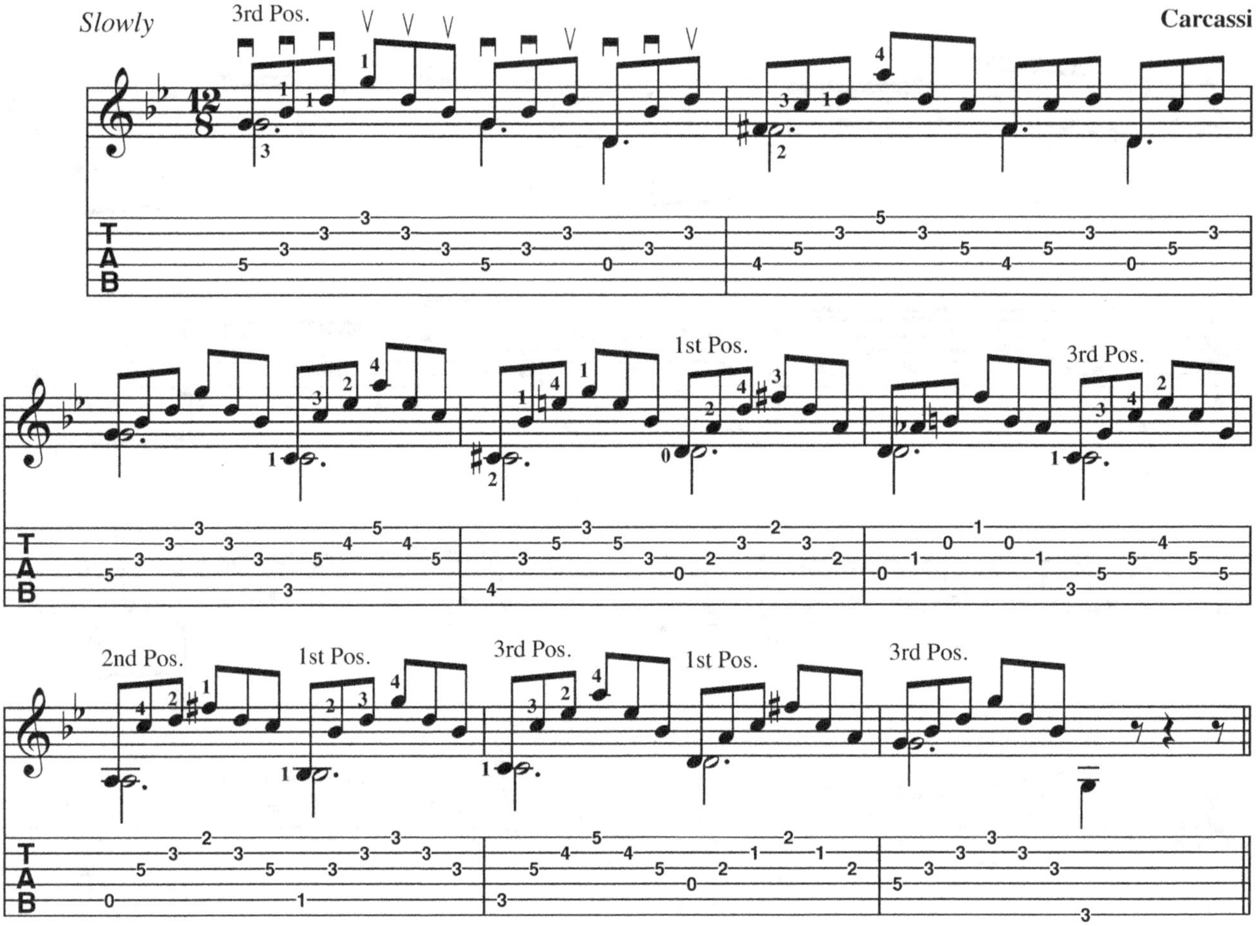

Andante in Bm

Allegro Brillante

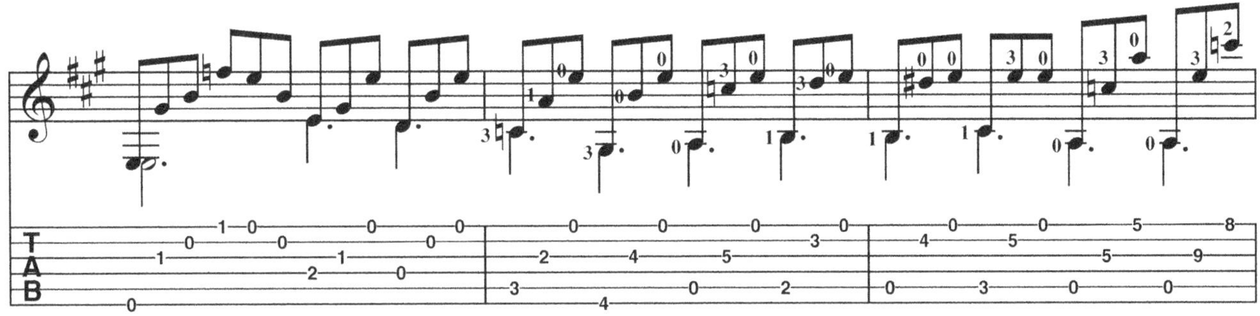

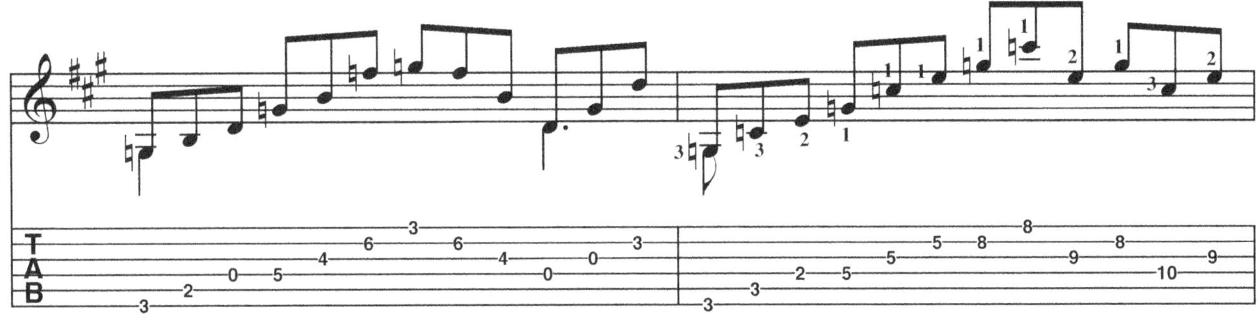

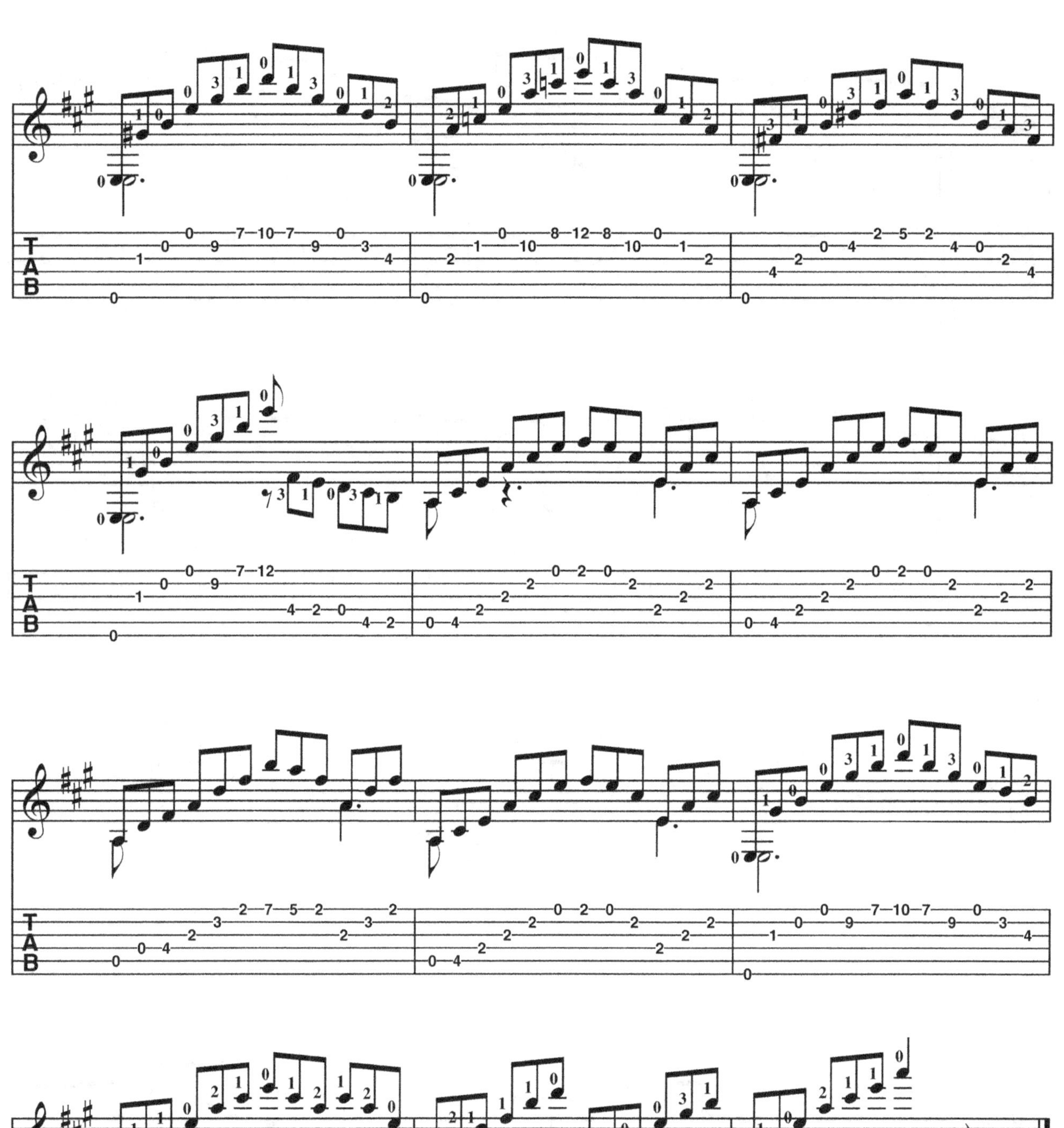

Meditation

Carcassi

Allegro

Use alternate picking
6th Pos.
Carcassi-Bay
Fine

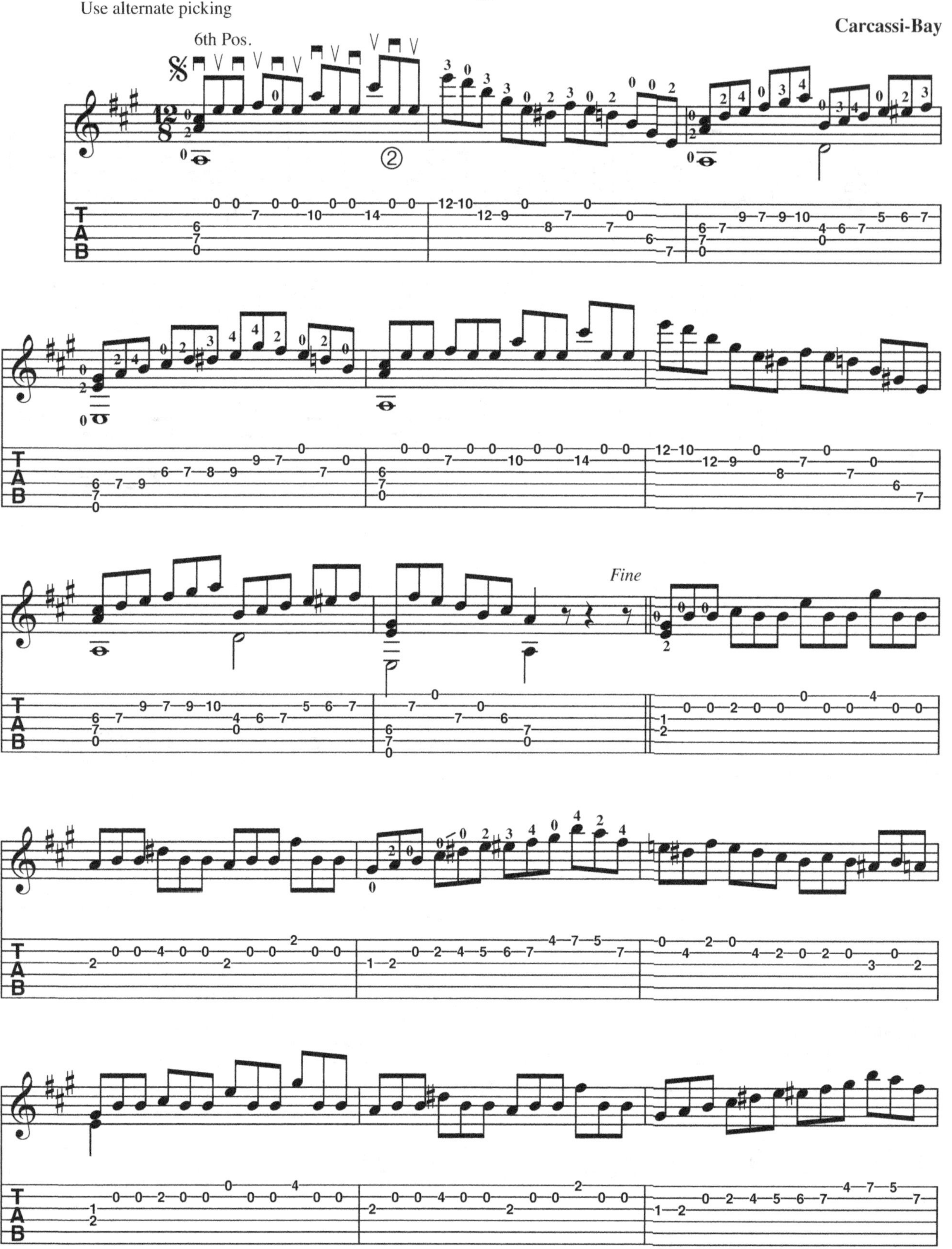

8th Pos.
D.S. al Fine
rit.

Study #2

Carcassi

2nd Pos.

poco rit.

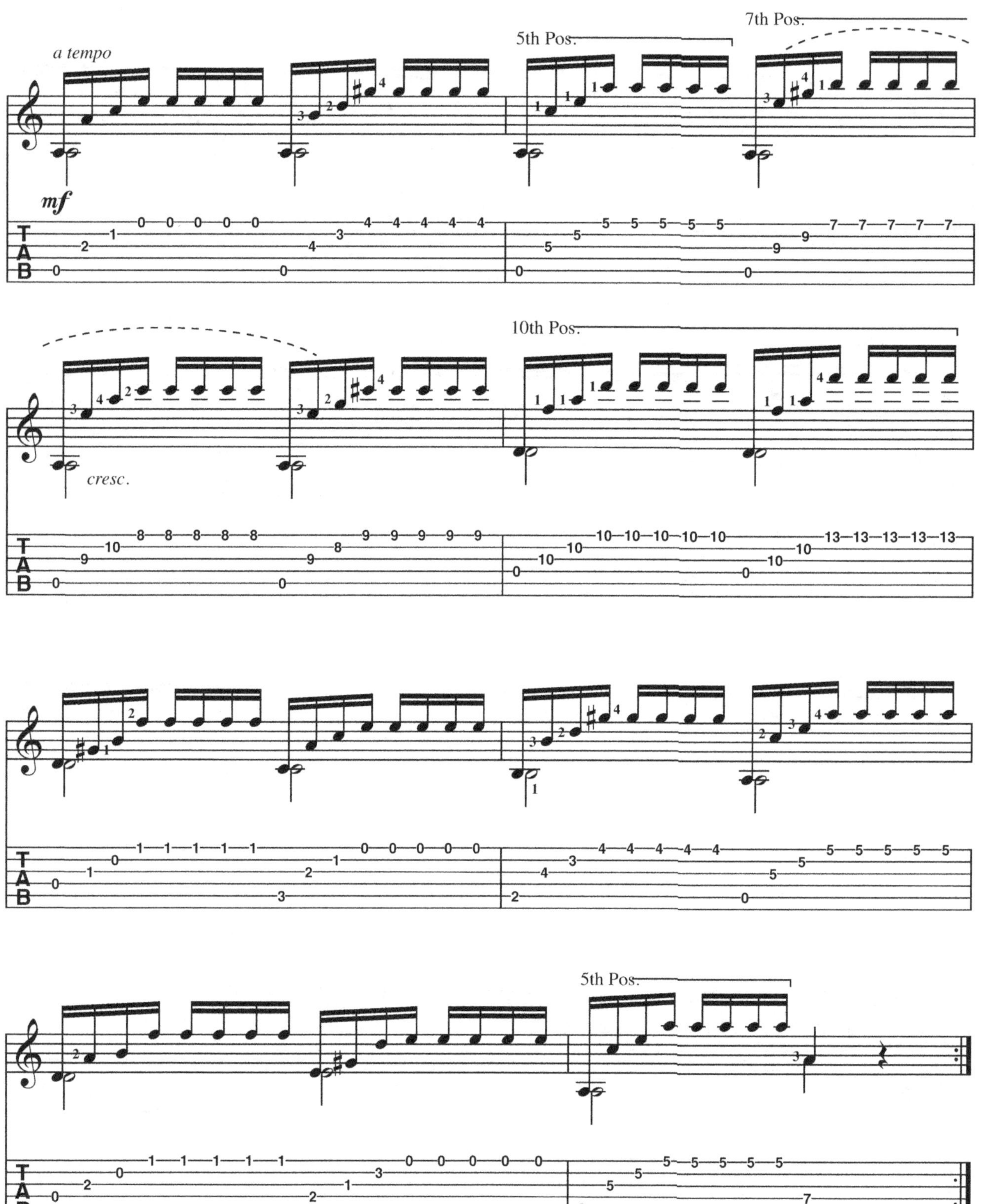

Prelude in C Minor

Study #5

Carcassi
7th Pos.
7th Pos.
20

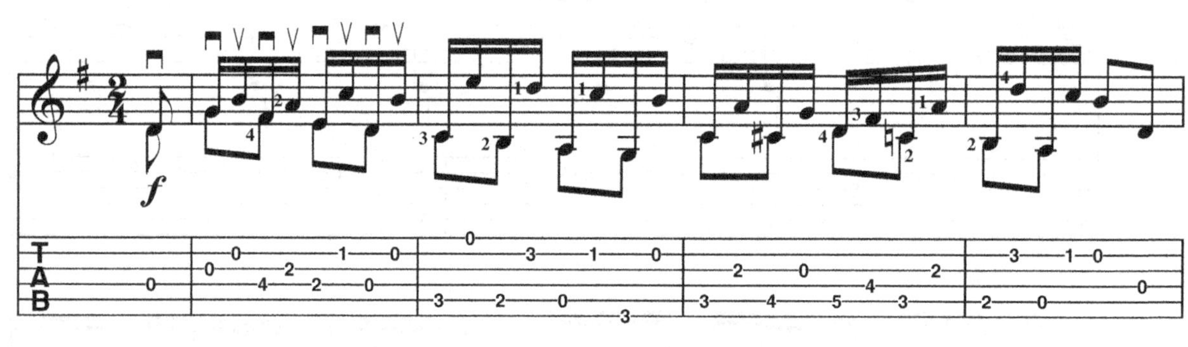

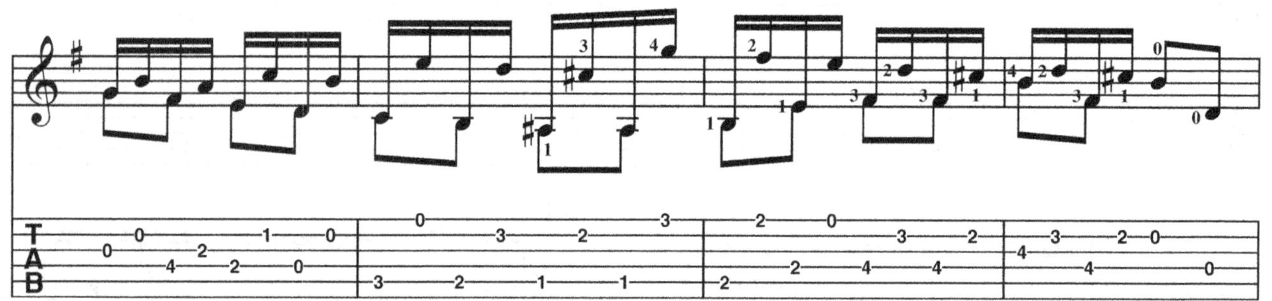

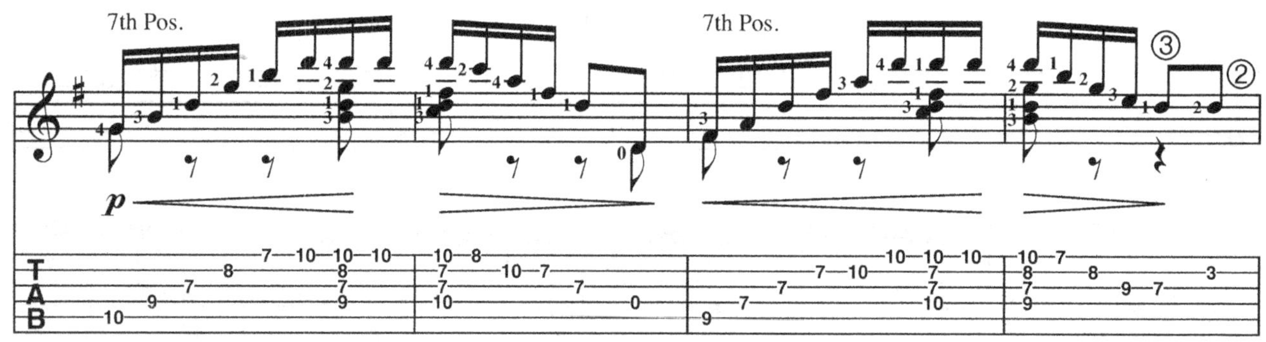

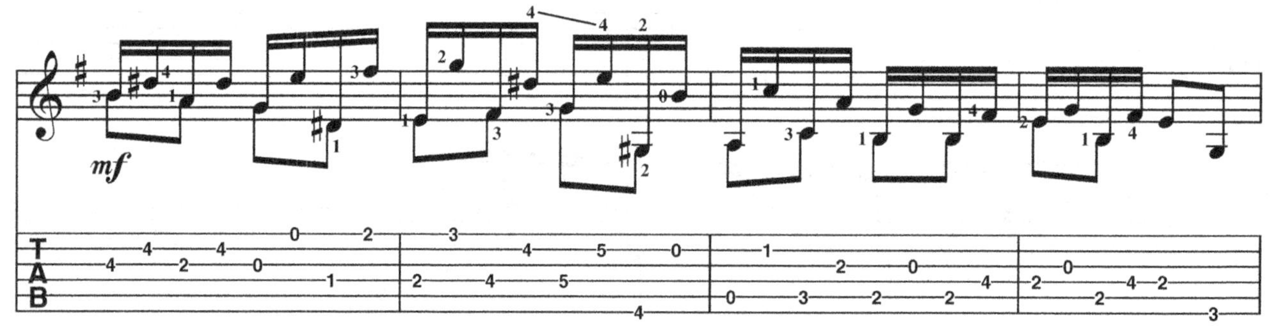

Prelude #5

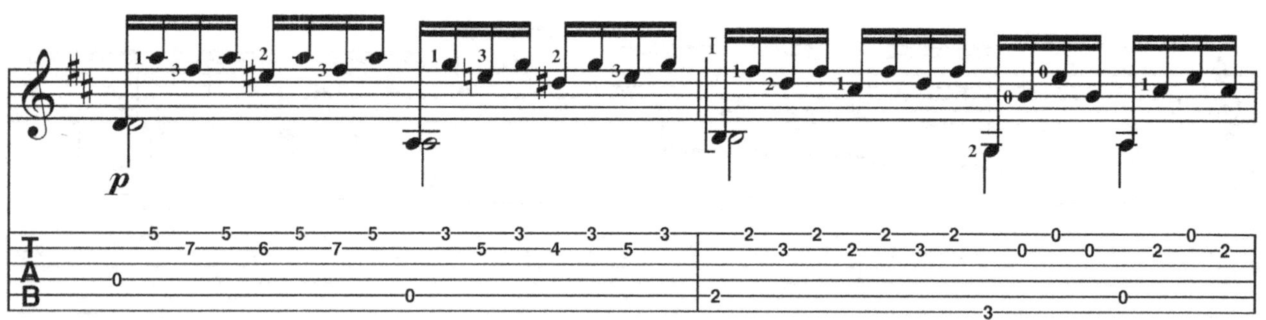

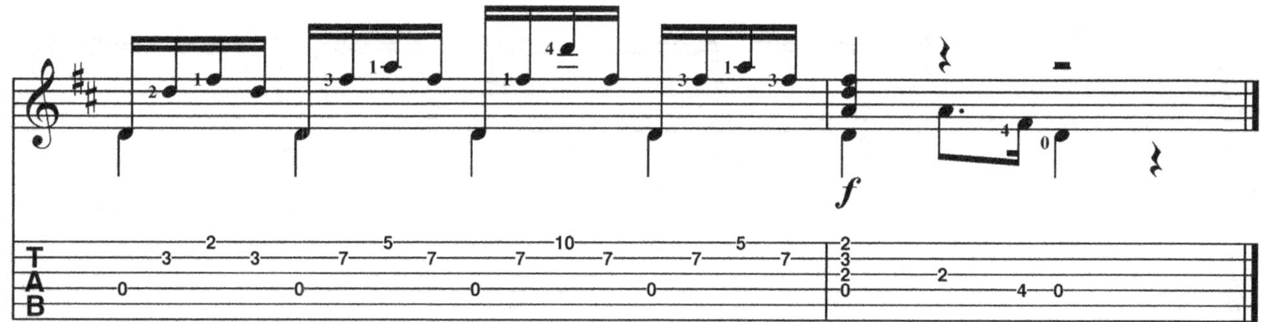

Etude in G Minor

Le Petite Moulin

rit.

Study #1

Scherzando
Harry Volpe
cresc.
dim.
mf
vibrato

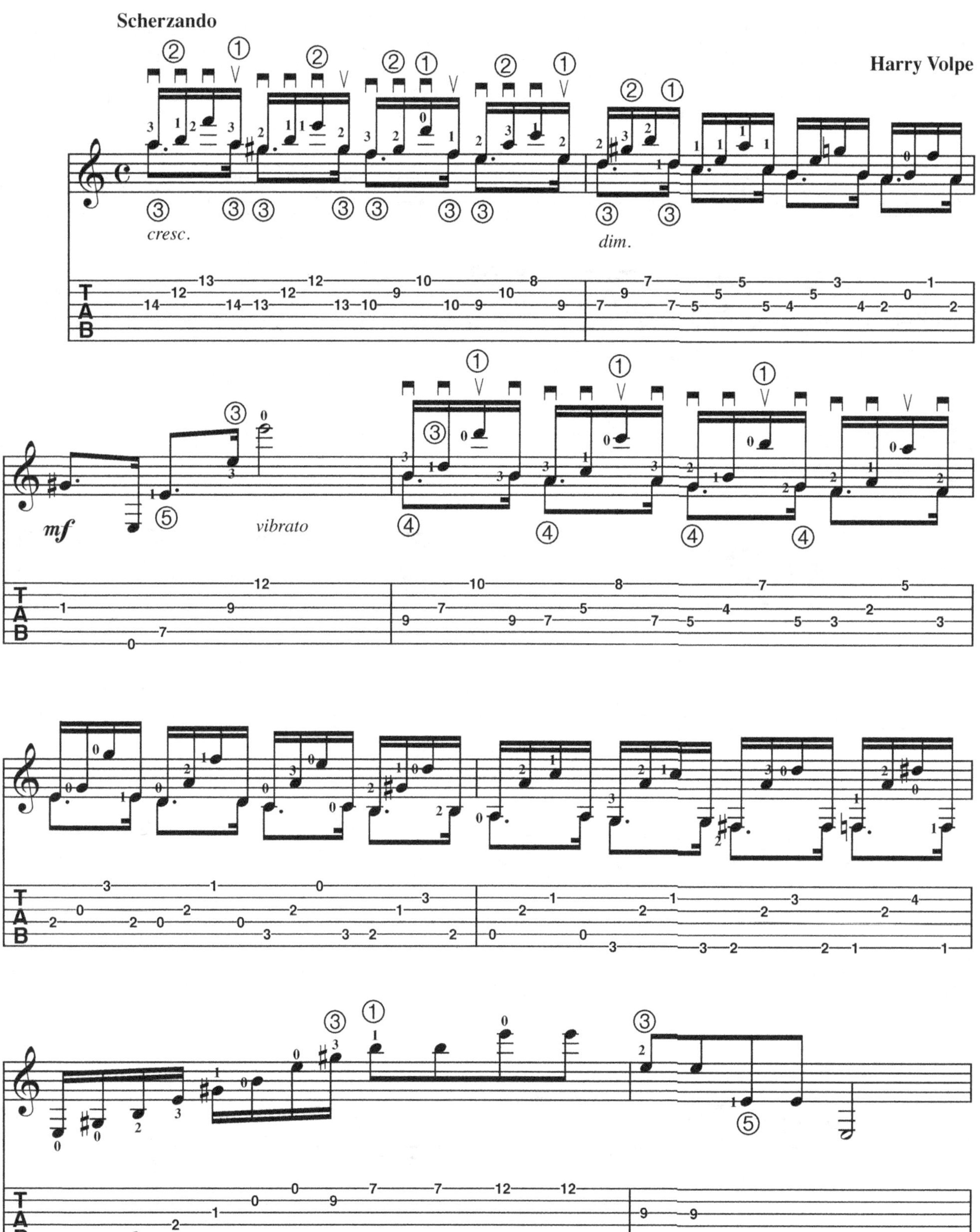

Moderato
p
mf
dolce
p
f
ff
f
ff

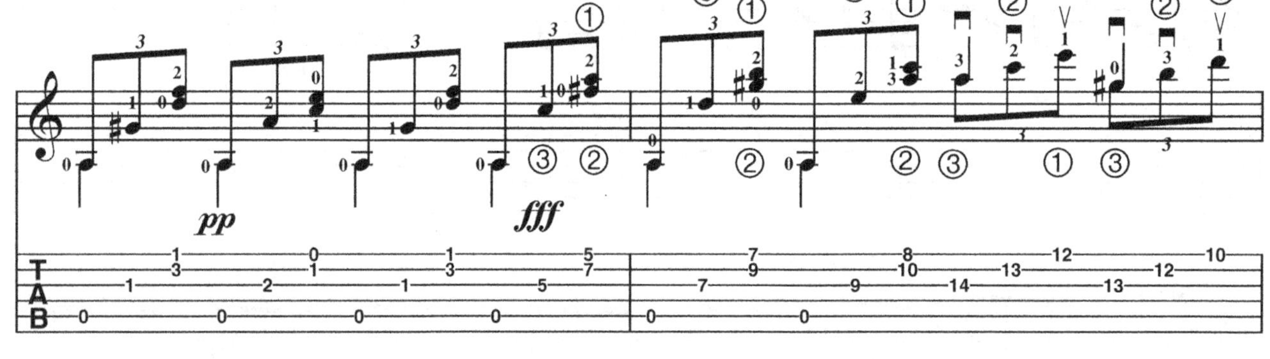
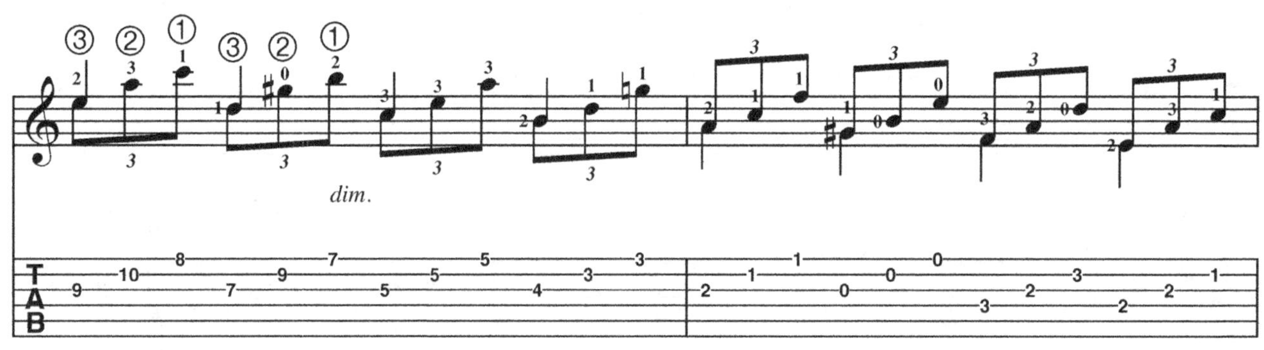
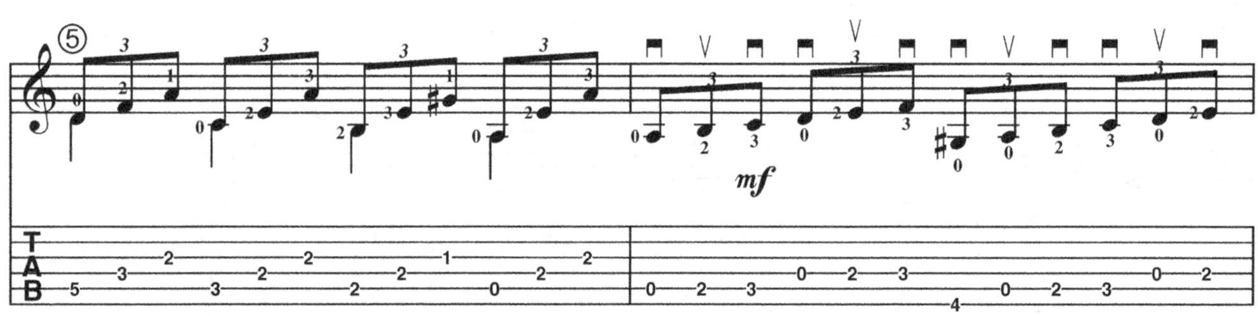

Study #8

Carcassi-Bay

2nd Pos.
BII

BVII
BIV

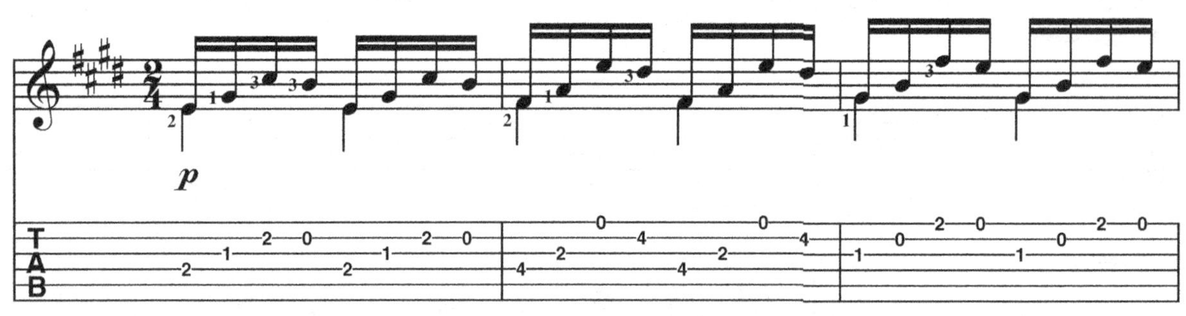

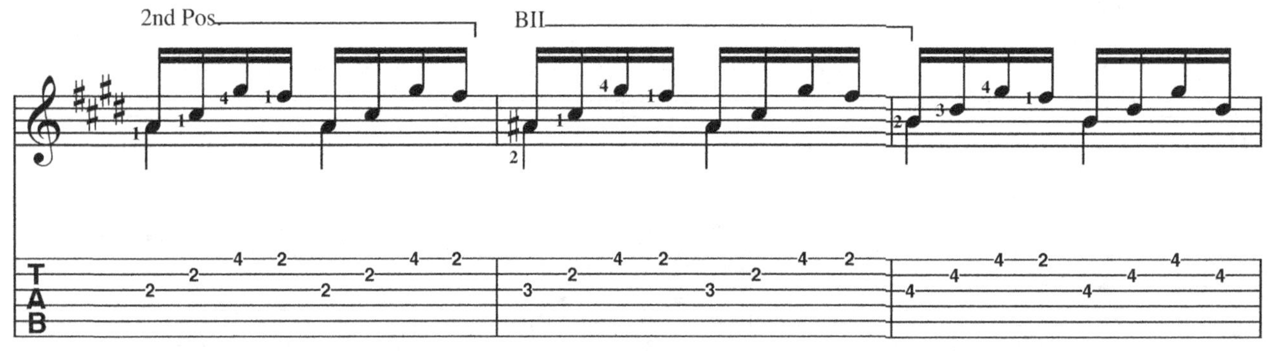

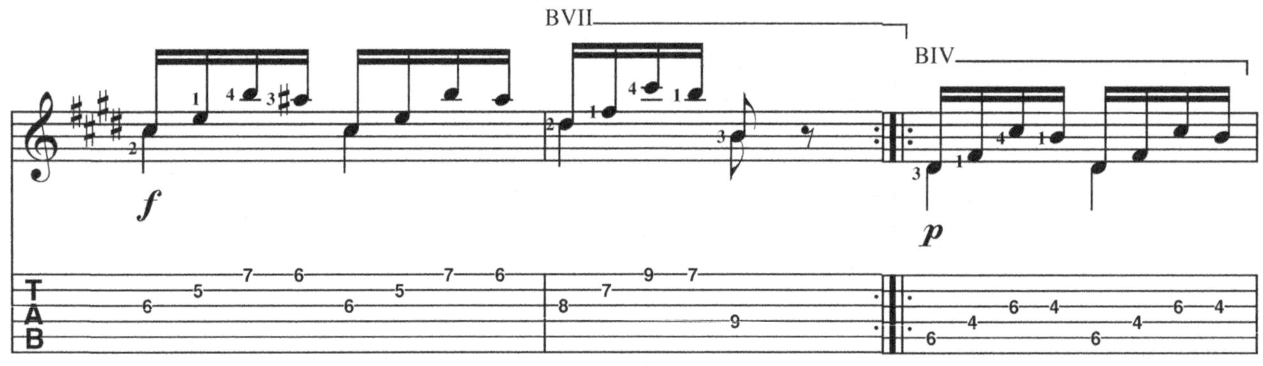

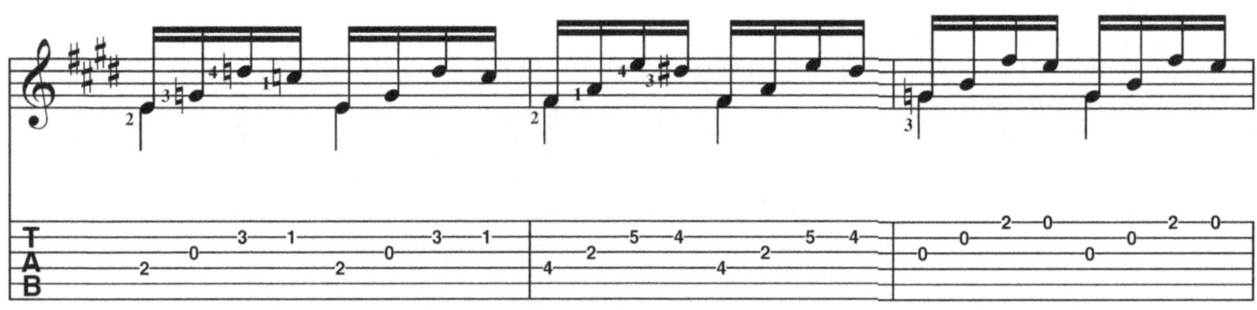

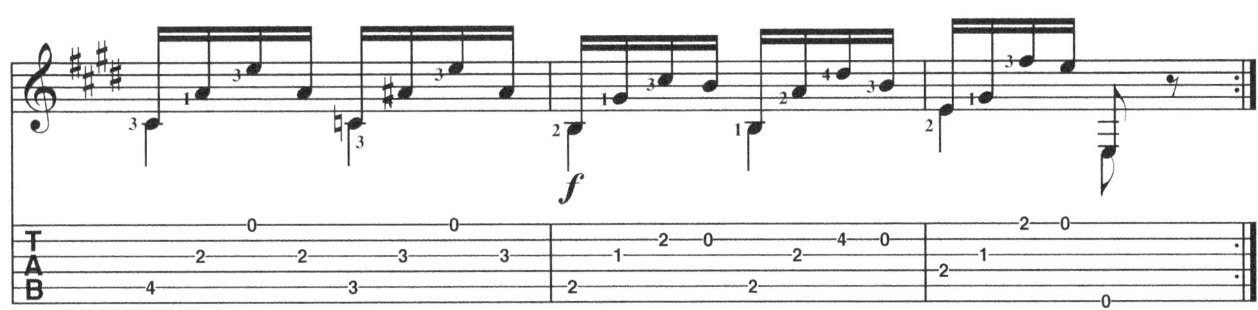

Study #15

Carcassi-Bay

mf
6th Pos.
f
8th Pos.
5th Pos.
p

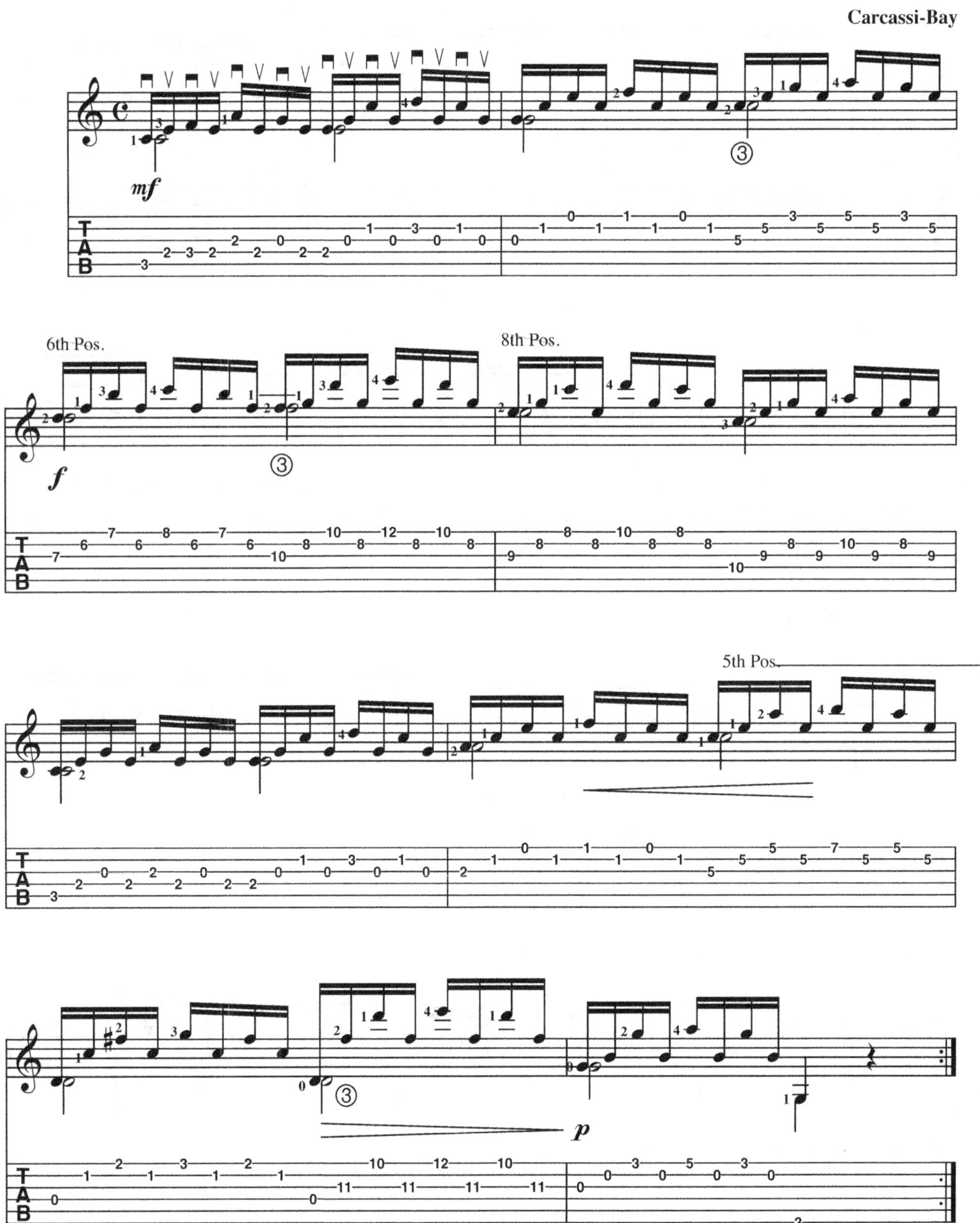

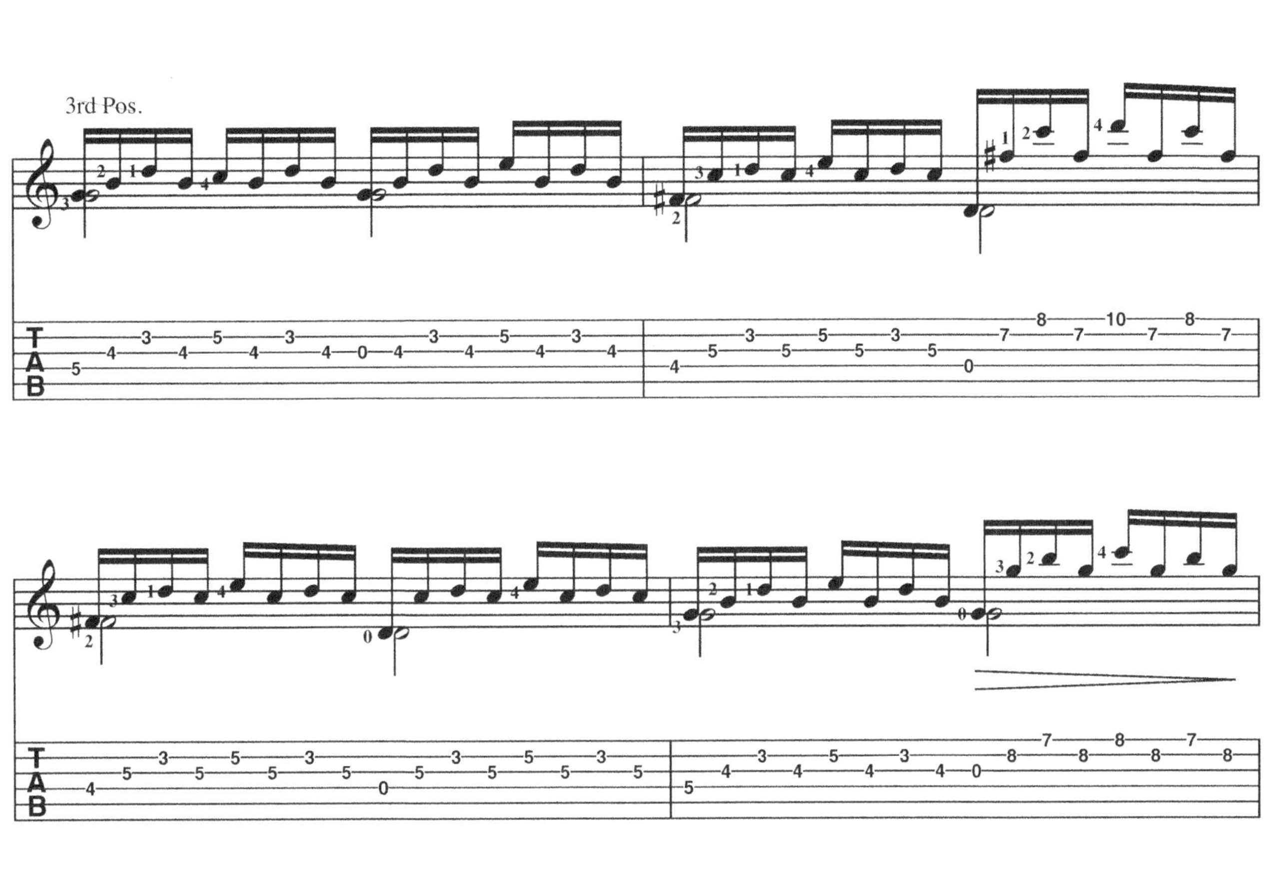

3rd Pos.

f

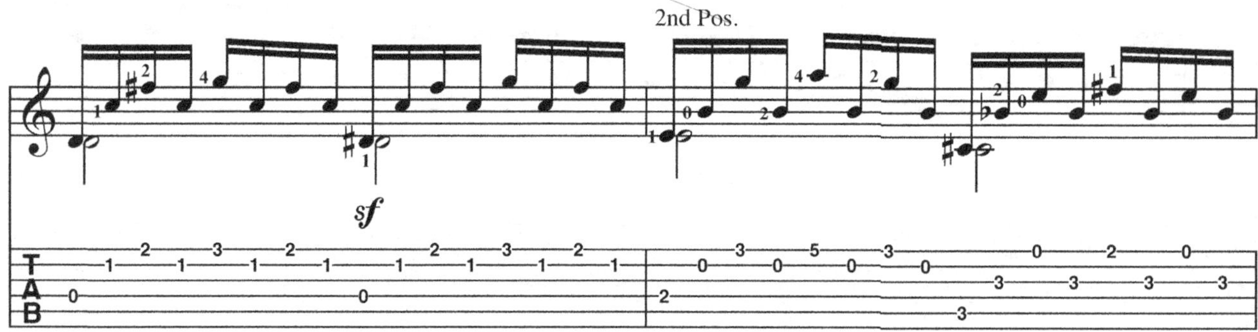
2nd Pos.
sf

f
rit.

a tempo
③

5th Pos.

4th Pos.
④

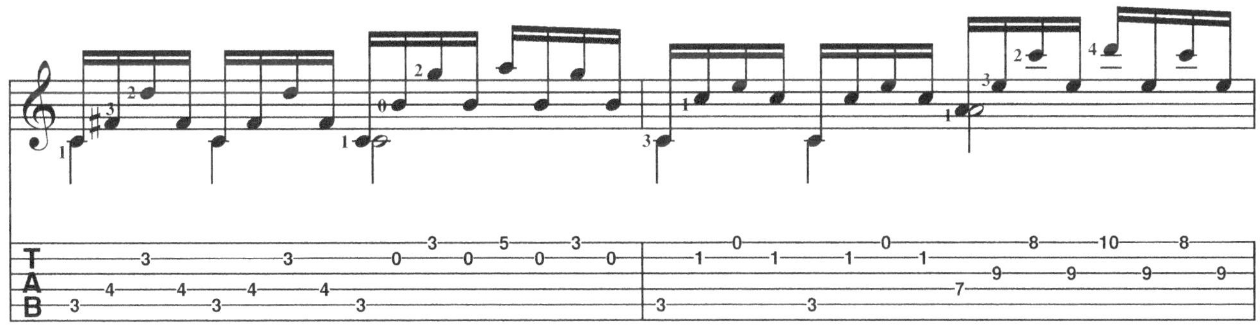

7th Pos.
8th Pos.

Study #22

Carcassi-Bay

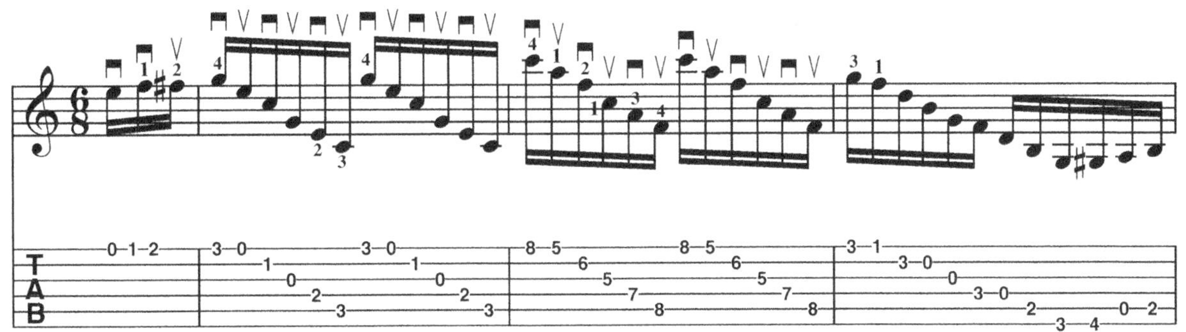

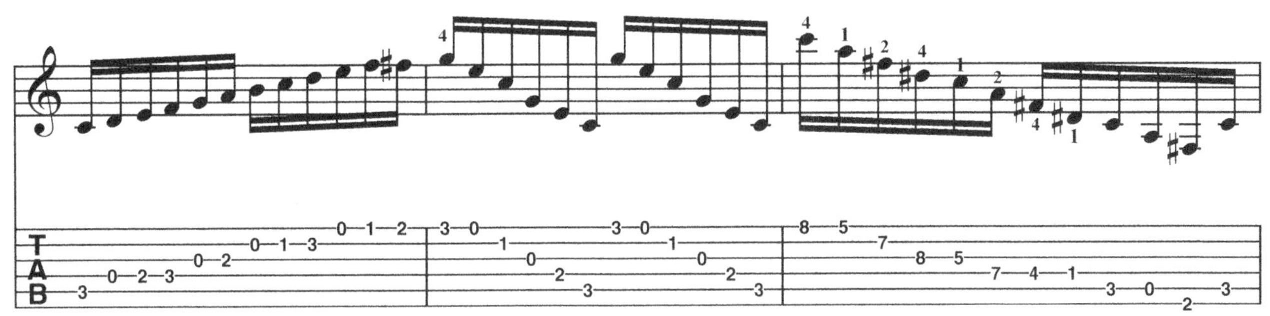

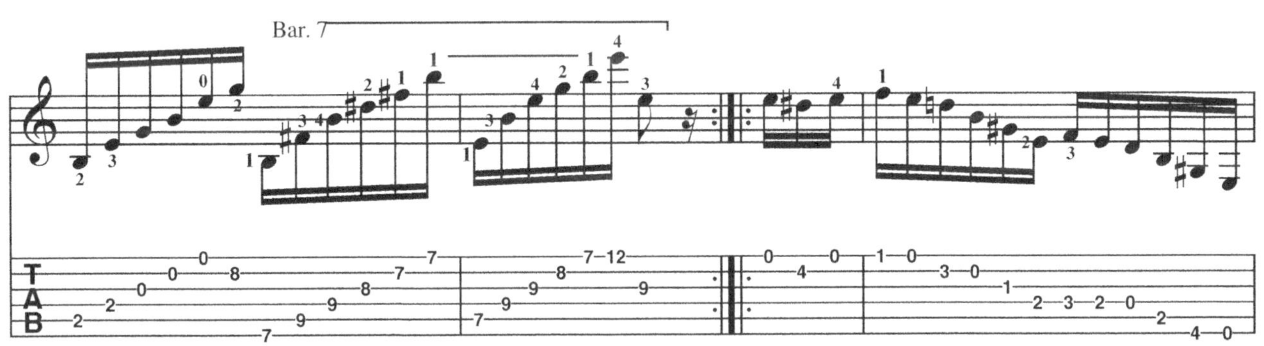

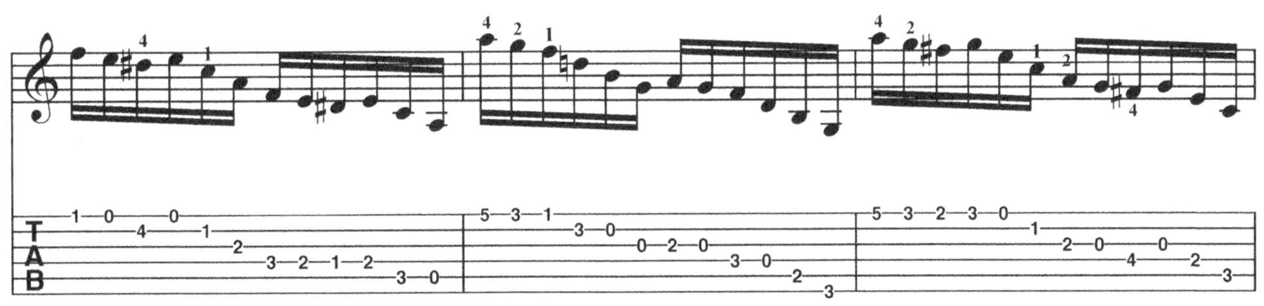

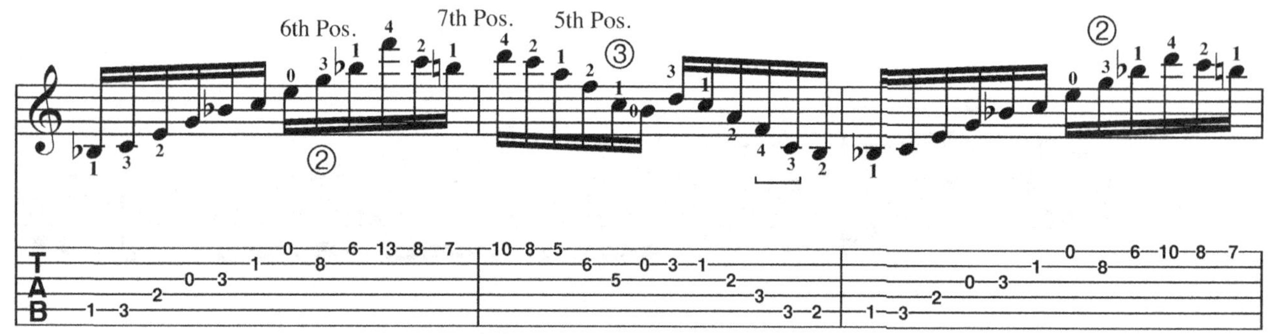

6th Pos.
7th Pos.
5th Pos.

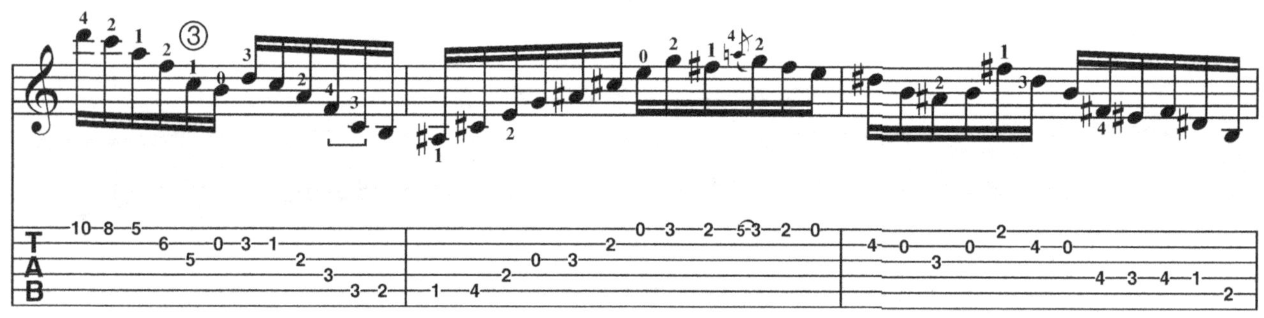

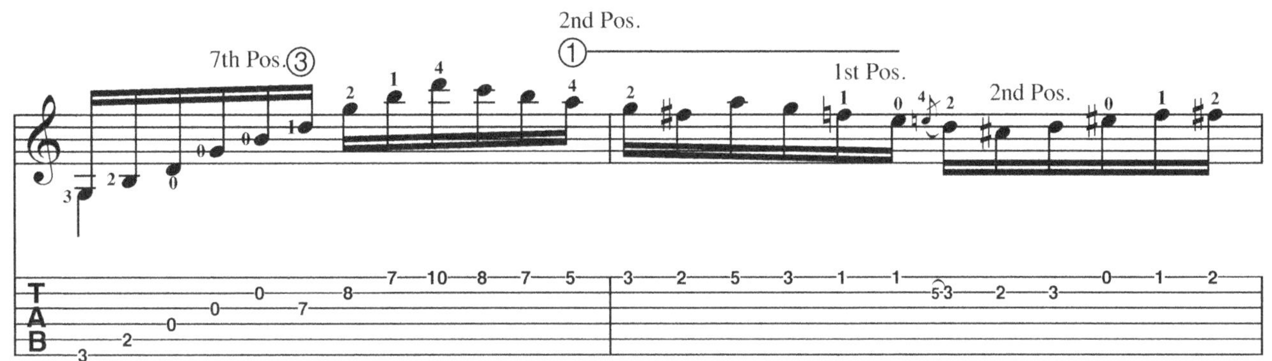

7th Pos.
2nd Pos.
1st Pos.
2nd Pos.

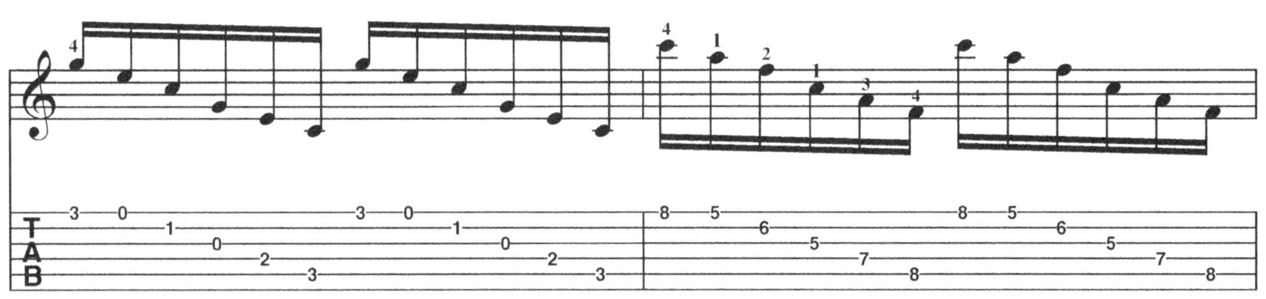

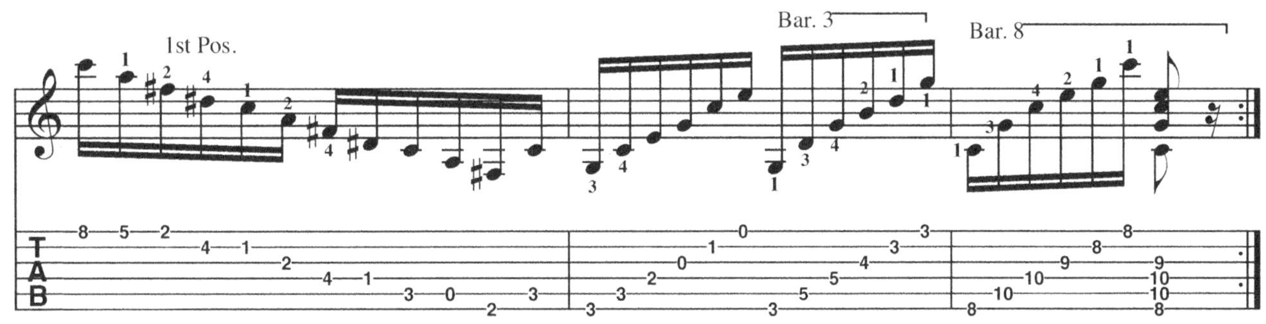

1st Pos.
Bar. 3
Bar. 8

Narcissus

Nevin-Bay

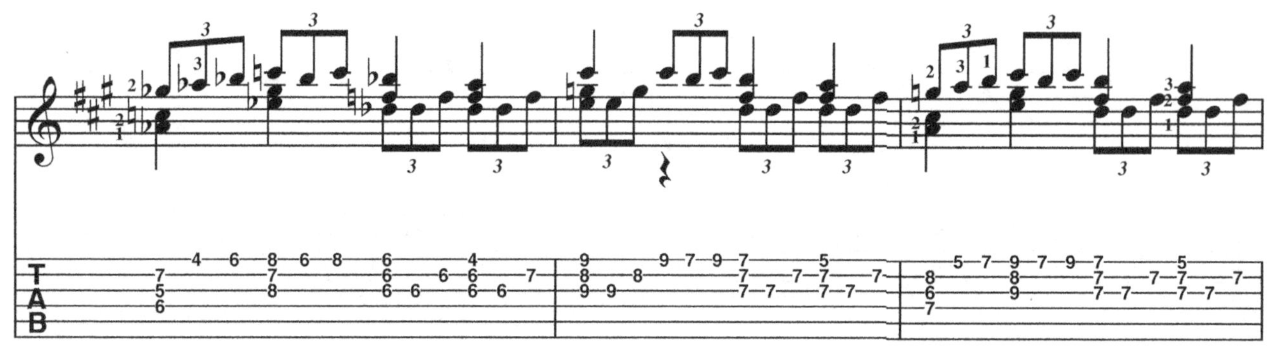

3
3
3
3
3
3

B♭
A♭
3
3
3
3
3
3
3
3
3
3
3
3
3
3

G
3
3
3
3
3
3
3
3
3
3
3

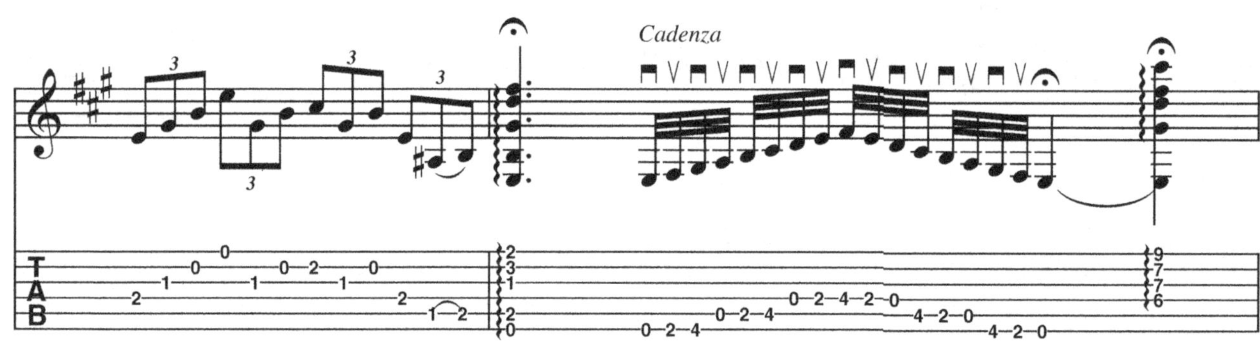

3
3
3
3
Cadenza

snap
snap
snap
snap
snap
Hold chord
rit.

UNIQUELY INTERESTING MUSIC!

Made in the USA
Monee, IL
07 July 2026

56550054R00031